110 Quilted Potholders

by Rita Weiss & Linda Causee

LEISURE ARTS, INC.
Little Rock, Arkansas

Produced by

Production Team

Creative Directors: Jean Leinhauser and Rita Weiss
Photography: Carol Wilson Mansfield
Book Design: Linda Causee
Technical Editor: Ann Harnden
Block Diagrams: April McArthur

Published by

LEISURE ARTS
the art of everyday living
www.leisurearts.com

©2013 by Leisure Arts, Inc., P. O. Box 55595, Little Rock, Arkansas 72215. All rights reserved. This publication is protected under federal copyright laws. Reproduction or distribution of this publication or any other Leisure Arts publication, including publications which are out of print, is prohibited unless specifically authorized. This includes, but is not limited to, any form of reproduction or distribution on or through the Internet, including posting, scanning or e-mail transmission.
We have made every effort to ensure that these instructions are accurate and complete. We cannot, however, be responsible for human error, typographical mistakes, or variations in individual work.

Library of Congress Control Number: 2013944417
ISBN-13: 978-1-4647-1241-8

ON THE COVERS
Potholders shown on front cover were made in alternate fabrics using the following patterns (clockwise from top left): Totem (page 54), Jacob's Ladder (page 50), Toad in the Puddle (page 44), Thrift (page 4), Tulip (page 36), and End of the Road (page 57).

Potholders shown on back cover (left to right, from top): Empire State (page 39), Hole in the Barn Door (page 38), Eternal Triangle (page 22), Tulip (page 36), Old Maid's Ramble (page 26), Triangles and Stripes (page 29), Enclosed Stars (page 23), Yankee Puzzle (page 34), Stars and Squares (page 4), Brave World (page 17), Granny's Choice (page 41), Sailboat (page 8), and Crown and Star (page 43).

Introduction

Creating 110 potholders seemed liked a daunting project when we first began. We worried about finding 110 different patterns; however, it didn't take long for us to realize that between the two of us, we had more than 110 blocks in our archives.

So soon began a fun adventure!

Then we began to think, "Is anyone ever going to want to make 110 potholders?"

As we looked at our patterns, we realized that more than just a book of potholders, we had produced a book of 110 different 8" blocks, all of which could be used to make a variety of quilted projects like wall hangings, quilted garments, tablecloths, placemats…even quilts of all sizes.

All of the blocks use the same templates that appear on page 63. It doesn't matter if you make potholders or quilts. If you want an 8" x 8" square, just choose one (or more) of the blocks in this book, and you're on your way to creating an original quilted project. If you have forgotten how to make a potholder, or never knew how, have no worries. We tell you "How to Make a Potholder" on page 59.

So have fun choosing the quilt block you want to use, whether it's for making a simple potholder or a magnificent, king-size quilt.

Contents

Patterns	4
How to Make a Potholder	59
Pattern Templates	63
Index	64

Thrift

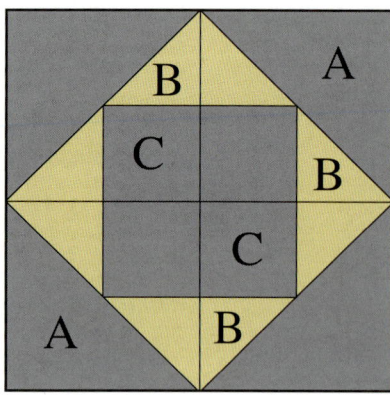

Templates and Fabric
4 A triangles, dk fabric
8 B triangles, lt fabric
4 C squares, dk fabric

Stars & Squares

Templates and Fabric
12 B triangles, lt fabric
12 B triangles, dk fabric
1 C square, lt fabric
8 D triangles, lt fabric
8 D triangles, dk fabric
4 E squares, lt fabric

Arkansas Crossroads

Templates and Fabric
- 4 B triangles, med fabric
- 4 B triangles, print fabric
- 4 C squares, dk fabric
- 4 C squares, med fabric
- 4 C squares, light fabic

Bachelor's Puzzle

Templates and Fabric
- 8 B triangles, dk fabric
- 8 B triangles, med fabric
- 8 B triangles, light fabric
- 4 C squares, light fabric

Anna's Choice

Road to Heaven

Templates and Fabric
16 B triangles, lt fabric
16 B triangles, dk fabric

Templates and Fabric
2 A triangles, med fabric
10 B triangles, dk fabric
6 B triangles, med fabric
4 C squares, lt fabric

The Anvil

Templates and Fabric
- 2 A triangles, dk fabric
- 2 A triangles, lt fabric
- 4 B triangles, dk fabric
- 4 B triangles, lt fabric
- 2 C squares, dk fabric
- 2 C squares, lt fabric

The Apple Tree

Templates and Fabric
- 7 B triangles, sky fabric
- 11 B triangles, tree fabric
- 11 D triangles, sky fabric
- 3 D squares, trunk fabric
- 7 E squares, apple fabric
- 13 E squares, sky fabric
- 1 E square, trunk fabric

Road to Oklahoma

Templates and Fabric

4 B triangles, lt fabric
4 B triangles, dk fabric
6 C squares, lt fabric
6 C squares, dk fabric

Sailboat

Templates and Fabric

4 B triangles, sail fabric
2 B triangles, boat fabric
4 B triangles, sky fabric
2 B triangles, water fabric
4 C squares, water fabric
2 C squares, boat fabric
4 C squares, sky fabric

Windblown Square

Templates and Fabric
8 B triangles, med fabric
8 B triangles, dk fabric
16 B triangles, lt fabric

Rocky Mountain Puzzle

Templates and fabric
10 B triangles, dk fabric
10 B triangles, lt fabric
2 C squares, lt fabric
12 E squares, dk fabric
4 E squares, lt fabric

Hour Glass

Templates and Fabric
16 B triangles, dk fabric
16 B triangles, lt fabric

Mrs. Smith's Favorite

Templates and Fabric
1 C square, lt fabric
16 D triangles, dk fabric
16 D triangles, lt fabric
20 E squares, lt fabric
24 E squares, dk fabric

Royal Star

Templates and Fabric

12 B triangles, lt fabric
4 B triangles, dk fabric
4 C squares, dk fabric
8 G triangles, dk fabric
8 G triangles, lt fabric

Blockade

Templates and Fabric

12 B triangles, lt fabric
10 B triangles, med fabric
10 B triangles, dk fabric

Basket of Scraps

Templates and Fabric

2 B triangles, flower fabric 1
2 B triangles, flower fabric 2
2 B triangles, flower fabric 3
2 B triangles, flower fabric 4
3 B triangles, dk fabric
5 B triangles, med fabric
1 C square, dk fabric
7 C squares, med fabric

Old Maid's Puzzle

Templates and Fabric

12 B triangles, lt fabric
16 B triangles, dk fabric
4 B triangles, med fabric

Northern Lights

Templates and Fabric
- 2 A triangles, dk fabric
- 4 B triangles, dk fabric
- 4 B triangles, lt fabric
- 6 C squares, lt fabric
- 2 C squares, dk fabric

Chinese Puzzle

Templates and Fabric
- 6 B triangles, dk fabric
- 9 B triangles, med fabric
- 9 B triangles, lt fabric
- 4 G triangles, dk fabric
- 4 G triangles, lt fabric
- 2 C squares, med fabric

Geometric

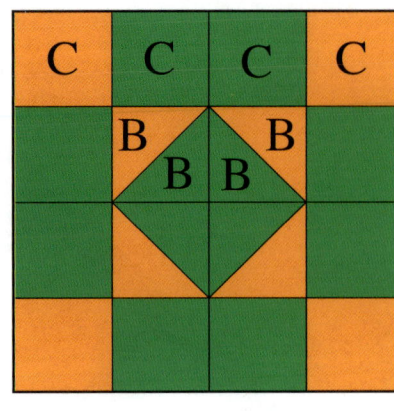

Templates and Fabric

4 B triangles, lt fabric
4 B triangles, dk fabric
8 C squares, dk fabric
4 C squares, lt fabric

Devil's Claw

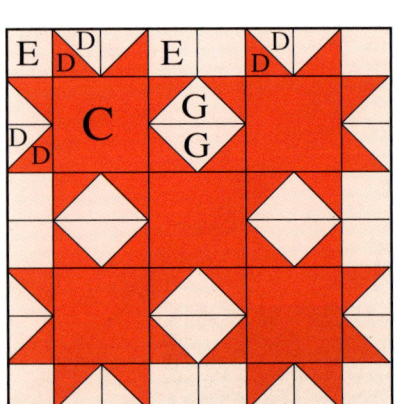

Templates and Fabric

5 C squares, dk fabric
32 D triangles, dk fabric
16 D triangles, lt fabric
12 E squares, lt fabric
8 G triangles, lt fabric

Buzzard's Roost

Templates and Fabric
2 A triangles, lt fabric
12 B triangles, lt fabric
12 B triangles, dk fabric

Mosaic

Templates and Fabric
16 B triangles, dk fabric
16 B triangles, lt fabric

Simple Flower Basket

Templates and Fabric
- 1 A triangle, dk fabric
- 1 A triangle, lt fabric
- 2 B triangles, dk fabric
- 6 B triangles, med fabric
- 8 B triangles, lt fabric
- 4 C squares, lt fabric

Churn Dash

Templates and Fabric
- 2 A triangles, dk fabric
- 8 B triangles, dk fabric
- 8 B triangles, lt fabric
- 4 C squares, dk fabric

Brave World

Templates and Fabric
4 A triangles, med fabric
8 B triangles, lt fabric
4 C squares, dk fabric

Georgetown Circle

Templates and Fabric
4 B triangles, very dk fabric
4 B triangles, dk fabric
4 C squares, lt fabric
4 G triangles, very dk fabric
12 G triangles, dk fabric
8 G triangles, med fabric
8 G triangles, lt fabric

Ribbons

Templates and Fabric

4 A triangles, dk fabric
8 B triangles, med fabric
8 B triangles, lt fabric

Chevrons

Templates and Fabric

8 B triangles, dk fabric
8 B triangles, med fabric
16 B triangles, lt fabric

Coxey's Army

Necktie

Templates and Fabric

4 B triangles, lt fabric
4 C squares, dk fabric
4 F strips, dk fabric
4 F strips, med fabric
4 G triangles, med fabric
4 G triangles, dk fabric

Templates and Fabric

4 A triangles, dk fabric
2 B triangles, dk fabric
2 B triangles, lt fabric
6 C squares, lt fabric

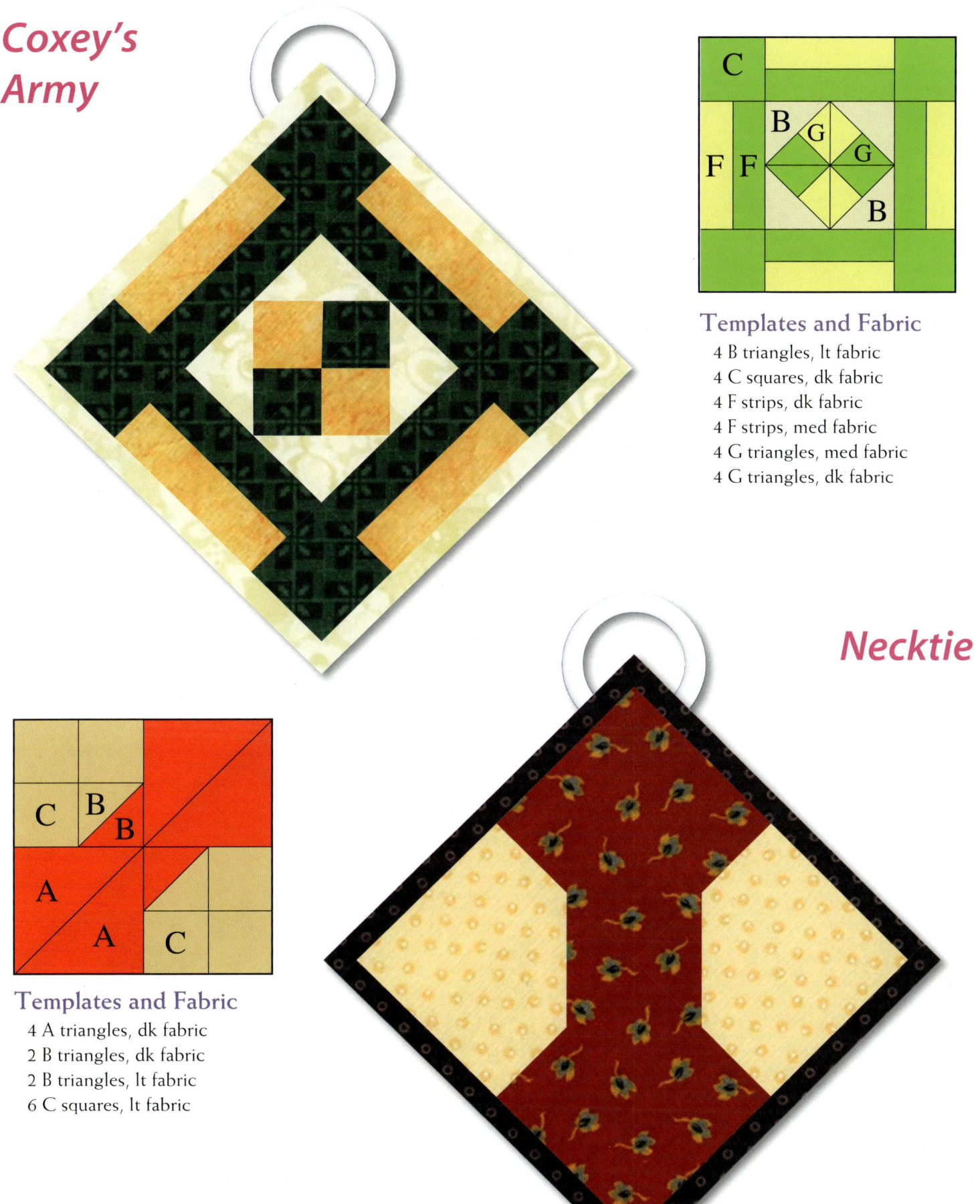

Next-Door Neighbor

Templates and Fabric
- 8 B triangles, med fabric
- 2 B triangles, very dk fabric
- 8 B triangles, dk fabric
- 6 B triangles, lt fabric
- 4 C squares, dk fabric

July Fourth

Templates and Fabric
- 8 B triangles, dk fabric
- 12 B triangles, med fabric
- 4 B triangles, lt fabric
- 4 C squares, lt fabric

Clay's Choice

Templates and Fabric
- 8 B triangles, dk fabric
- 4 B triangles, med fabric
- 4 B triangles, lt fabric
- 4 C squares, lt fabric
- 4 C squares, med fabric

Return of the Swallows

Templates and Fabric
- 8 B triangles, dk fabric
- 8 B triangles, med fabric
- 16 B triangles, lt fabric

Eternal Triangle

Templates and Fabric

36 D triangles, lt fabric
36 D triangles, dk fabric
4 C squares, lt fabric
12 E squares, lt fabric

Wild Goose Chase

Templates and Fabric

2 A triangles, lt fabric
2 C squares, lt fabric
32 D triangles, lt fabric
12 G triangles, dk fabric
8 G triangles, med fabric
4 G triangles, lt fabric

End of Day

Templates and Fabric

4 B triangles, lt fabric
4 B triangles, med fabric
8 B triangles, dk fabric
4 C squares, med fabric
4 C squares, dk fabric

Enclosed Stars

Templates and Fabric

40 D triangles, dk fabric
64 D triangles, lt fabric
24 D triangles, med fabric

Friendship

Templates and Fabric

1 A triangle, red fabric
1 A triangle, green fabric
1 A triangle, yellow fabric
1 A triangle, blue fabric
12 B triangles, white fabric
1 B triangle, red fabric
1 B triangle, green fabric
1 B triangle, yellow fabric
1 B triangle, blue fabric

Noon and Night

Templates and Fabric

12 B triangles, dk fabric
4 B triangles, lt fabric
4 C squares, lt fabric
8 G triangles, med fabric
8 G triangles, lt fabric

Eight-Pointed Star

Templates and Fabric
4 B triangles, very dk fabric
8 B triangles, lt fabric
4 B triangles, med dark fabric
4 C squares, lt fabric
16 G triangles, med fabric

Susannah

Templates and Fabric
4 B triangles, dk fabric
4 B triangles, lt fabric
4 C squares, dk fabric
4 C squares, lt fabric
4 C squares, med fabric

Old Maid's Ramble

Templates and Fabric

8 B triangles, lt fabric
4 B triangles, dk fabric
8 B triangles, med fabric
1 C square, dk fabric
20 G triangles, lt fabric

Broken Dishes

Templates and Fabric

16 B triangles, lt fabric
16 B triangles, dk fabric

Patience Corners

Railroad Crossing

Templates and Fabric

8 B triangles, very dk fabric
8 B triangles, dk fabric
8 B triangles, med fabric
8 B triangles, lt fabric

Templates and Fabric

10 B triangles, med fabric
12 B triangles, lt fabric
20 G triangles, dk fabric

Jack-in-the-Pulpit

Templates and Fabric
- 1 C square, black fabric
- 12 B triangles, red fabric
- 4 B triangles, brown fabric
- 4 B triangles, peach fabric
- 8 B triangles, lt fabric
- 4 G triangles, lt fabric

Diamond Star

Templates and Fabric
- 4 B triangles, green fabric
- 8 B triangles, lt fabric
- 1 C square, lt fabric
- 4 C squares, green fabric
- 16 D triangles, brown fabric
- 8 D triangles, lt fabric
- 8 E squares, brown fabric

Triangles and Stripes

Templates and Fabric

8 B triangles, med fabric
4 B triangles, dk fabric
1 C square, dk fabric
4 F strips, dk fabric
4 F strips, lt fabric
4 G triangles, lt fabric

Catch As You Can

Templates and Fabric

8 B triangles, lt fabric
4 B triangles, dk fabric
4 C squares, lt fabric
12 G squares, lt fabric
12 G squares, dk fabric

Depression

Templates and Fabric
64 D triangles, dk fabric
64 D triangles, lt fabric

Heart

Templates and Fabric
2 A triangles, dk fabric
2 A triangles, lt fabric
4 B triangles, dk fabric
4 B triangles, lt fabric
4 C squares, dk fabric

Pineapple

Templates and Fabric

2 B triangles, dk fabric
3 B triangles, med fabric
1 B triangle, lt fabric
5 B triangles, very lt fabric
2 C squares, dk fabric
6 C squares, med fabric
1 C square, lt fabric
1 C square, very lt fabric

The Butterfly

Templates and Fabric

12 B triangles, dk fabric
8 B triangles, med fabric
4 B triangles, lt fabric
8 B triangles, very lt fabric

Flying Fish

Templates and Fabric
- 8 C squares, lt fabric
- 16 D triangles, dk fabric
- 16 D triangles, med fabric
- 32 D triangles, lt fabric

Snail's Trail

Templates and Fabric
- 5 B triangles, dk fabric
- 5 B triangles, lt fabric
- 4 C squares, dk fabric
- 5 C squares, lt fabric
- 4 G triangles, dk fabric
- 4 G triangles, lt fabric

Sunlight and Shadow

Templates and Fabric

4 B triangles, lt fabric
4 B triangles, med fabric
8 B triangles, print fabric
4 C squares, lt fabric
2 C squares, print fabric
2 C squares, med fabric

Baby Bunting

Templates and Fabric

6 B triangles, med fabric
6 B triangles, lt fabric
2 C squares, dk fabric
6 C squares, med fabric
2 C squares, lt fabric

Yankee Puzzle

Templates and Fabric

12 B triangles, very dk fabric
4 B triangles, dk fabric
12 B triangles, med fabric
4 B triangles, lt fabric

Fancy Stripe

Templates and Fabric

10 B triangles, dk fabric
6 B triangles, med fabric
16 B triangles, lt fabric

Wild Waves

Crazy Ann

Templates and Fabric
- 16 B triangles, lt fabric
- 16 G triangles, lt fabric
- 16 G triangles, dk fabric

Templates and Fabric
- 8 B triangles, dk fabric
- 4 C squares, lt fabric
- 8 D triangles, med fabric
- 8 D triangles, lt fabric
- 12 E squares, med fabric
- 8 E squares, lt fabric
- 4 G triangles, lt fabric

Tulip

Templates and Fabric

- 2 B triangles, dk green fabric
- 2 B triangles, lt green fabric
- 4 B triangles, red fabric
- 2 B triangles, yellow fabric
- 2 B triangles, purple fabric
- 6 B triangles, lt fabric
- 5 C squares, dk green fabric
- 1 C square, lt green fabric
- 1 C square, lt fabric

Tea Leaf

Templates and Fabric

- 8 B triangles, lt fabric
- 8 B triangles, dk fabric
- 6 C squares, lt fabric
- 2 C squares, dk fabric

Shooting Squares

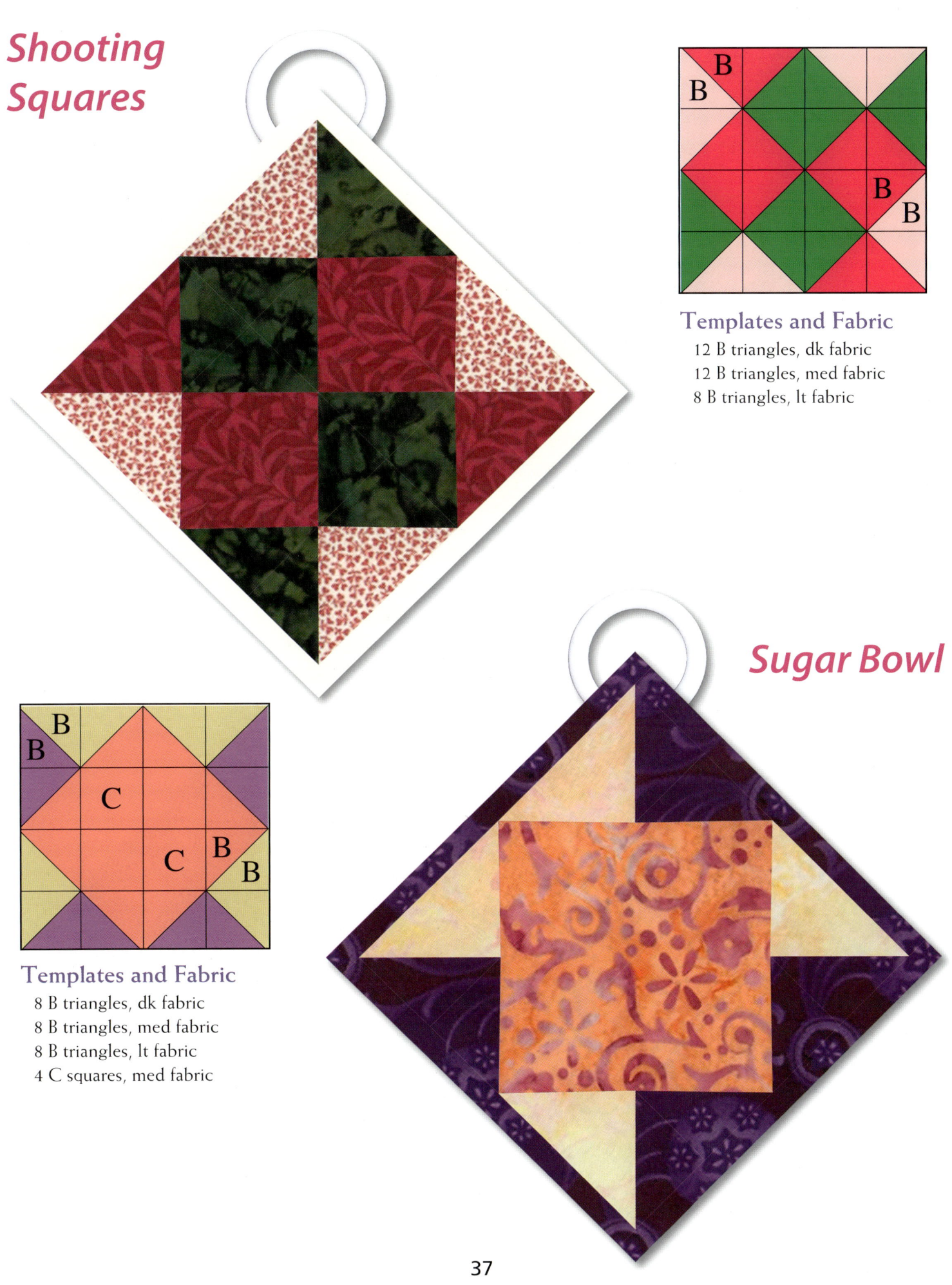

Templates and Fabric
12 B triangles, dk fabric
12 B triangles, med fabric
8 B triangles, lt fabric

Sugar Bowl

Templates and Fabric
8 B triangles, dk fabric
8 B triangles, med fabric
8 B triangles, lt fabric
4 C squares, med fabric

Hither and Yon

Hole in the Barn Door

Templates and Fabric
2 A triangles, very dk fabric
3 B triangles, very dk fabric
11 B triangles, lt fabric
1 C square, lt fabric
8 G triangle, dk fabric
8 G triangle, med fabric

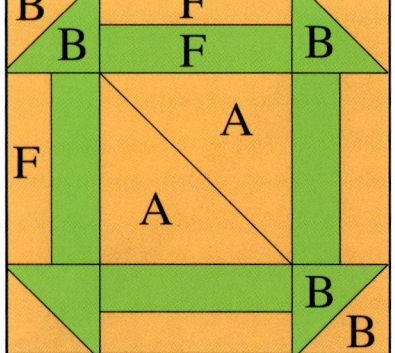

Templates and Fabric
2 A triangles, dk fabric
4 B triangles, lt fabric
4 B triangles, dk fabric
4 F strips, dk fabric
4 F strips, lt fabric

Sunny Lanes

Templates and Fabric
- 8 B triangles, med fabric
- 8 B triangles, very lt fabric
- 16 E squares, dk fabric
- 16 E squares, lt fabric

Empire State

Templates and Fabric
- 16 B triangles, dk fabric
- 16 B triangles, lt fabric

Balkan Puzzle

Templates and Fabric
16 B triangles, dk fabric
16 B triangles, lt fabric

Interwoven Puzzle

Templates and Fabric
40 D triangles, dk fabric
40 D triangles, lt fabric
24 E squares, lt fabric

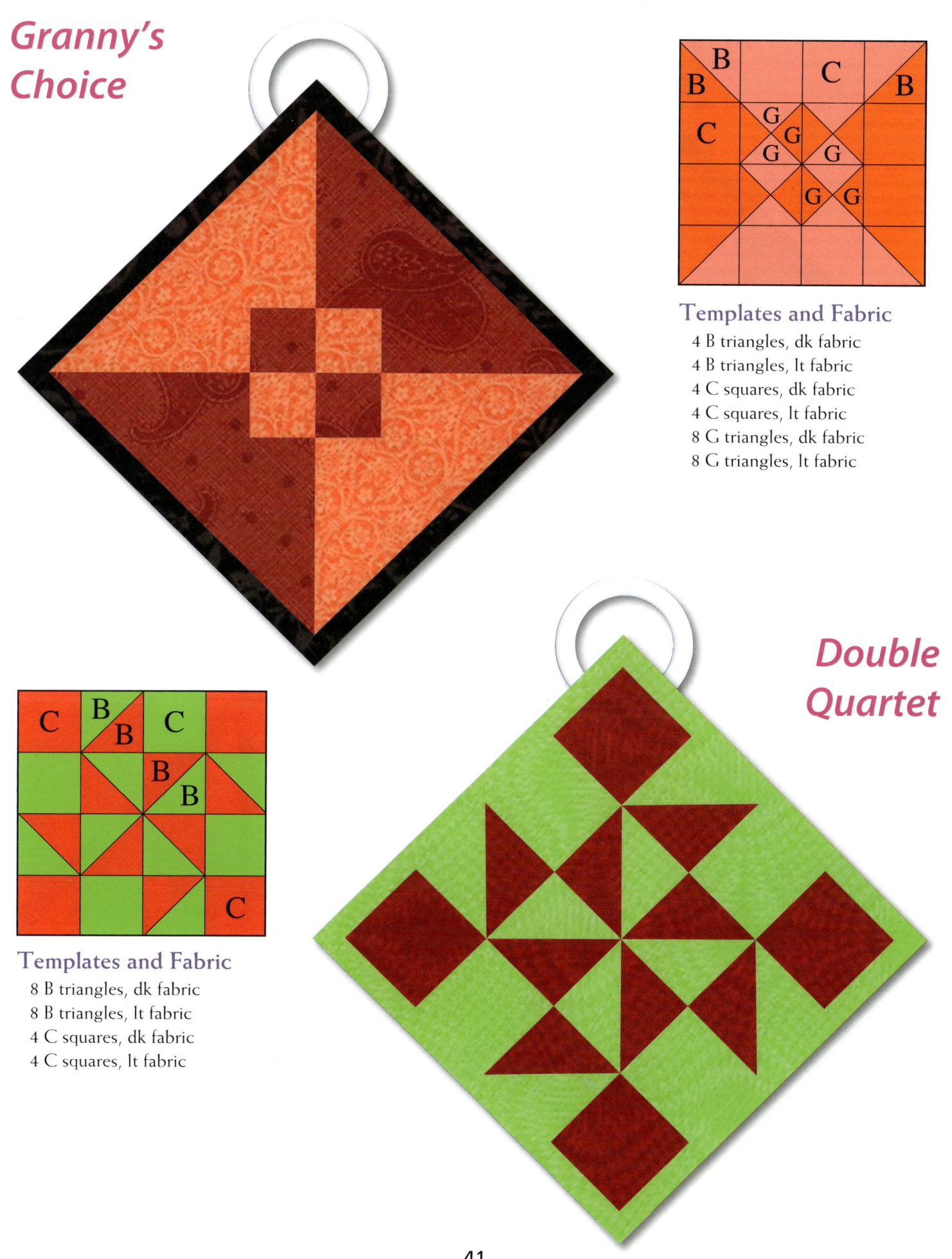

Granny's Choice

Templates and Fabric

- 4 B triangles, dk fabric
- 4 B triangles, lt fabric
- 4 C squares, dk fabric
- 4 C squares, lt fabric
- 8 G triangles, dk fabric
- 8 G triangles, lt fabric

Double Quartet

Templates and Fabric

- 8 B triangles, dk fabric
- 8 B triangles, lt fabric
- 4 C squares, dk fabric
- 4 C squares, lt fabric

Kansas Dugout

Templates and Fabric

16 D triangles, dk fabric
24 D triangles, med fabric
24 D triangles, lt fabric
16 E squares, med fabric
16 E squares, lt fabric

Mrs. Taft's Choice

Templates and Fabric

6 B triangles, dk fabric
8 B triangles, med fabric
10 B triangles, lt fabric
2 C squares, dk fabric
2 C squares, lt fabric

Crown and Star

Templates and Fabric
4 C squares, lt fabric
1 C square, dk fabric
24 D triangles, dk fabric
24 D triangles, lt fabric
12 E squares, lt fabric
8 E squares, dk fabric

Whirlwind

Templates and Fabric
4 A triangles, dk fabric
8 B triangles, lt fabric
8 B triangles, dk fabric

Toad in the Puddle

Templates and Fabric
- 4 B triangles, lt blue fabric
- 4 B triangles, green fabric
- 12 B triangles, very lt fabric
- 1 C square, lt blue fabric
- 8 G triangles, dk fabric
- 8 G triangles, green fabric
- 4 G triangles, very lt fabric

Criss Cross

Templates and Fabric
- 8 B triangles, dk fabric
- 12 B triangles, med fabric
- 8 B triangles, lt fabric
- 2 C squares, lt fabric

Shoo-Fly

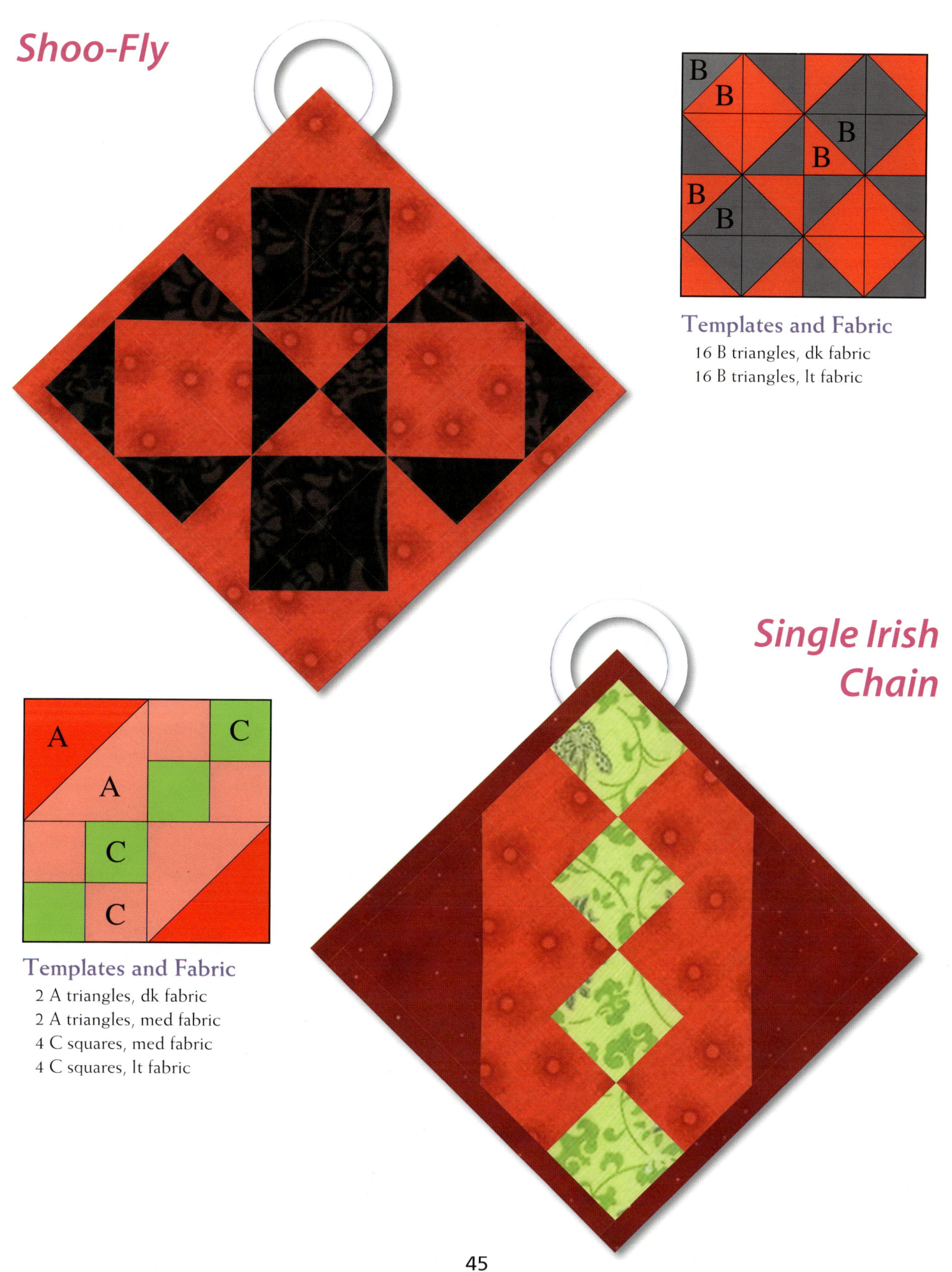

Templates and Fabric
16 B triangles, dk fabric
16 B triangles, lt fabric

Single Irish Chain

Templates and Fabric
2 A triangles, dk fabric
2 A triangles, med fabric
4 C squares, med fabric
4 C squares, lt fabric

Original Block

Stepping Stones

Templates and Fabric
16 B triangles, dk fabric
16 B triangles, lt fabric

Templates and Fabric
16 D triangles, dk fabric
16 D triangles, lt fabric
8 E squares, very dk fabric
8 E squares, dk fabric
8 E squares, med fabric
24 E squares, lt fabric

Double Pinwheel

Templates and Fabric
4 A triangles, dk fabric
8 B triangles, med fabric
8 C triangles, lt fabric

Twelve Triangles

Templates and Fabric
4 A triangles, very lt fabric
8 B triangles, dk fabric
4 B triangles, med fabric
4 B triangles, lt fabric

Delectable Mountains

Templates and Fabric
4 B triangles, lt fabric
2 B triangles, dk fabric
32 D triangles, dk fabric
28 D triangles, lt fabric
10 E squares, dk fabric
12 E squares, lt fabric

Lucky Pieces

Templates and Fabric
4 B triangles, very dk fabric
8 B triangles, dk fabric
4 B triangles, med fabric
4 B triangles, very lt fabric
12 B triangles, lt fabric

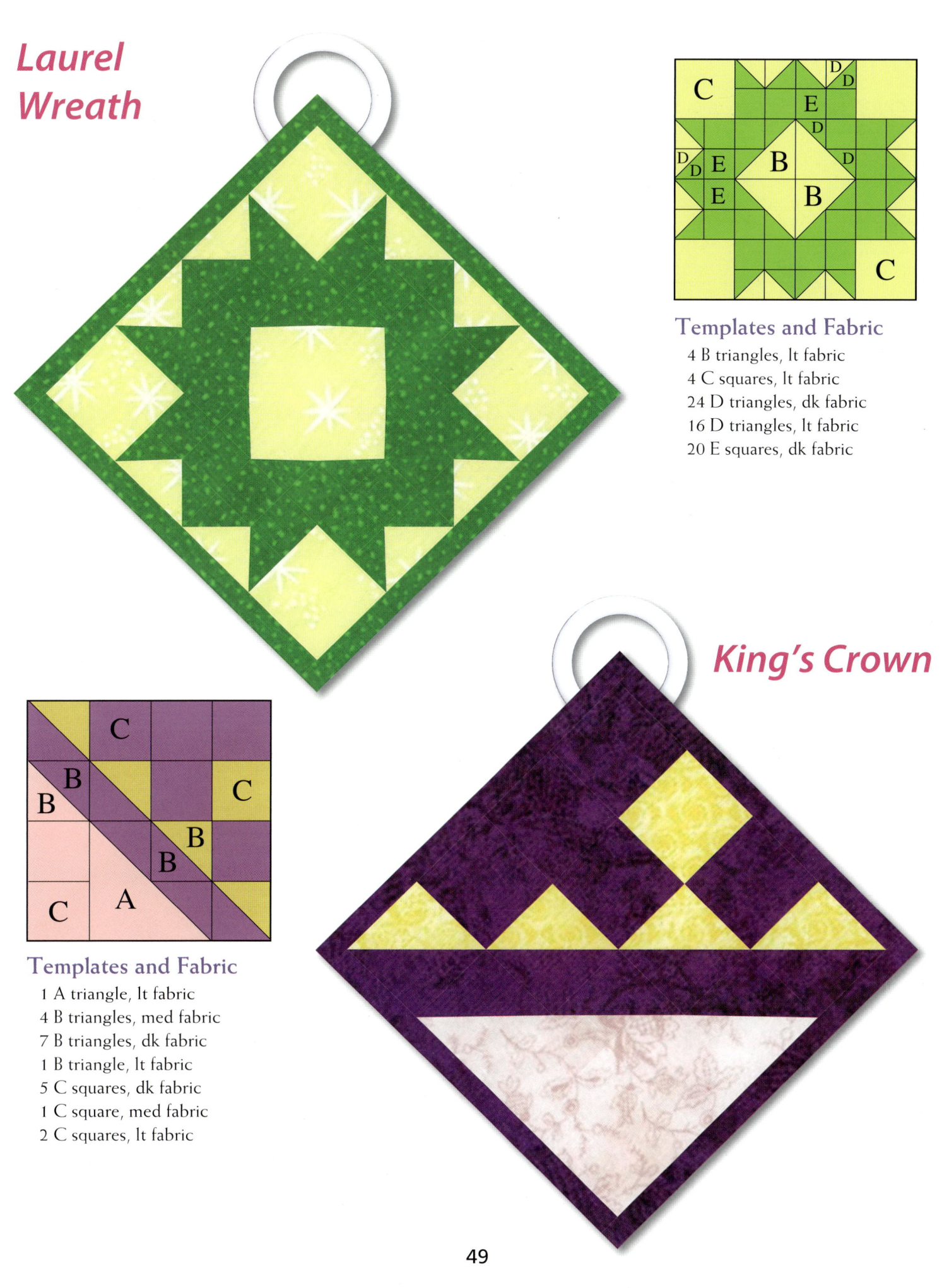

Laurel Wreath

Templates and Fabric

4 B triangles, lt fabric
4 C squares, lt fabric
24 D triangles, dk fabric
16 D triangles, lt fabric
20 E squares, dk fabric

King's Crown

Templates and Fabric

1 A triangle, lt fabric
4 B triangles, med fabric
7 B triangles, dk fabric
1 B triangle, lt fabric
5 C squares, dk fabric
1 C square, med fabric
2 C squares, lt fabric

Shadow Boxes

Templates and Fabric
- 4 A triangle, lt fabric
- 4 B triangles, dk fabric
- 8 B triangles, med fabric
- 4 B triangles, very lt fabric

Jacob's Ladder

Templates and Fabric
- 8 B triangles, med fabric
- 8 B triangles, lt fabric
- 16 E squares, dk fabric
- 16 E squares, very lt fabric

Pinwheels

Templates and Fabric
- 4 B triangles, lt fabric
- 4 B triangles, med fabric
- 4 C squares, lt fabric
- 4 C squares, med fabric
- 4 C squares, dk fabric

Windmill

Templates and Fabric
- 8 B triangles, dk fabric
- 8 B triangles, med fabric
- 4 C squares, med fabric
- 4 C squares, lt fabric

White House Steps

Lily

Templates and Fabric
- 24 E squares, lt fabric
- 40 E squares, dk fabric

Templates and Fabric
- 4 B triangles, dk fabric
- 16 D triangles, lt fabric
- 20 D triangles, dk fabric
- 12 E squares, lt fabric
- 8 E squares, dk fabric
- 8 G triangles, lt fabric
- 10 G triangles, med fabric

Ocean Waves

Templates and Fabric
- 8 B triangles, med fabric
- 48 D triangles, lt fabric
- 48 D triangles, dk fabric

Flower Basket

Templates and Fabric
- 1 B triangle, flower fabric 1
- 1 B triangle, flower fabric 2
- 1 B triangle, flower fabric 3
- 1 B triangle, flower fabric 4
- 1 B triangle, flower fabric 5
- 1 B triangle, flower fabric 6
- 10 B triangles, lt fabric
- 4 B triangles, dk fabric
- 5 C squares, lt fabric
- 1 C square, dk fabric

Totem

Templates and Fabric

3 A triangles, dk fabric
8 B triangles, med fabric
2 B triangles, lt fabric
5 C squares, lt fabric

Wheels

Templates and Fabric

14 B triangles, dk fabric
10 B triangles, med fabric
8 B triangles, lt fabric

Star of the West

Templates and Fabric

16 B triangles, lt fabric
16 B triangles, dk fabric

Ribbon Star

Templates and Fabric

12 B triangles, dk fabric
12 B triangles, lt fabric
4 C Squares, lt fabric

Winged Star

Templates and Fabric

8 B triangles, dk fabric
8 B triangles, med fabric
16 B triangles, lt fabric

Pinwheel Askew

Templates and Fabric

8 B triangles, lt fabric
8 B triangles, dk fabric
8 C squares, dk fabric

End of the Road

Templates and Fabric

12 B triangles, dk fabric
12 B triangles, lt fabric
2 F strips, dk fabric
2 F strips, lt fabric

Linked Stars

Templates and Fabric

1 C square, very dk fabric
1 C square, dk fabric
4 C squares, lt fabric
8 D triangles, very dk fabric
8 D triangles, dk fabric
16 D triangles, lt fabric
8 E squares, med fabric
16 E squares, lt fabric

Streak of Lightning

Templates and Fabric
- 4 A triangles, lt fabric
- 4 A triangles, dk fabric

Nelson's Victory

Templates and Fabric
- 4 B triangles, lt fabric
- 4 B triangles, med fabric
- 4 C squares, lt fabric
- 4 C squares, med fabric
- 4 C squares, dk fabric

HOW TO MAKE A POTHOLDER

The blocks used to make any of these potholders have a finished size of 8" x 8". After adding a ¼" binding around all four edges, the completed potholder will measure 8½" x 8½". The individual blocks can also be used any time you might want an 8" block for another quilting project—even for a full-size quilt.

Supplies for Making a Potholder

Small amounts of contrasting cotton fabrics
9½" square of cotton backing fabric
one 2½"-wide x 40" fabric strip (for binding)
three 9½" squares of batting
template material
plastic or metal ring approximately 1" in diameter (for hanging)

Fabrics for the Potholder, Binding and Backing

For hundreds of years, quilts were made with 100% cotton fabric, and this remains today the fabric of choice for most quilters. There are many properties in cotton that make it especially well suited for sewing potholders as well as quilts. Since your potholder will be subjected to heat, the fact that cotton can withstand heat makes it the best fabric for potholders. Many other fabrics, such as polyesters, have a very low tolerance for heat and will probably not be suitable for a potholder.

There are other properties in cotton as well that make it well suited for potholders. There is less distortion in cotton fabric, thereby affording greater security in making certain that even the smallest bits of fabric will fit together. Since potholders will probably need to be washed frequently, most cottons are colorfast and shrink resistant. If you are unsure of your fabric, you may want to pre-test all fabric.

To test your fabric, cut a strip about 2" wide from each piece of fabric that you will use in your potholder. Measure both the length and the width of the strip. Then immerse the strip in a bowl of very hot water, using a separate bowl for each piece of fabric. If the fabric bleeds, it might be a good idea to choose another fabric. Then take one of the strips and iron it dry with a very hot iron. Now measure it and compare it to the original strip to determine if the fabric is shrinking. If all of your fabric is shrinking the same amount, there will probably be no problem, but just to make sure, eliminate the fabric that is shrinking.

Cotton works very well for the backing fabric as well. Some quilters like to use non-flammable fabrics like those used for ironing board covers for the backing.

Batting

In order to make your potholder thick enough to protect the hands from the heat, you should use at least three layers of cotton batting.

Templates

All of the templates used to make the potholders in this book are on page 63. The required templates are listed with each pattern. You just need to decide which potholder you wish to make.

You can then trace or photocopy the templates of your choice. Then glue the templates onto plastic or heavy cardboard. When you are certain that your glue has dried, cut out your templates. If your templates become worn, simply repeat the process. If you are planning to do your piecing by machine, cut out your templates on the broken line. If you are piecing by hand, cut out your templates on the solid lines. The seam allowances for hand piecing will be added later when you cut out the pieces. It's always a good idea to write the template's letter in the center of the template. Since many of the potholders use the same pattern pieces, if you copy and prepare all of the templates, you can make every potholder in this book.

Cutting

For Machine Piecing

Lay the template (with the ¼" seam allowance added) on the **wrong** side of the fabric near the top left edge of the material but not on the selvage, placing it so that as many straight sides of the piece as possible are parallel to the crosswise and lengthwise grain of the fabric. Trace around the template with a marking tool such as a hard lead pencil. This will be your cutting line; use a sharp scissors or a rotary cutter and cut accurately.

The traditional seam allowance in quilting is ¼" so be certain that you sew each seam with a ¼" seam allowance. After you have joined two pieces together, press the seams flat to one side, not open.

For Hand Piecing

Lay the template, cut on the solid lines, on the fabric as described on page 59 for Machine Piecing. Trace around the template with your marking tool. This will be your stitching line.

Now measure ¼" around this shape. With a ruler, draw this second line which is your cutting line. The seam allowance does not have to be perfect since it will not show, but the stitching line must be perfectly straight or the pieces will not fit together.

Sewing

Before you begin to sew the block, lay out all of the pieces you will need for the block. Then sew the pieces for the individual patterns first **(Fig. 1)**.

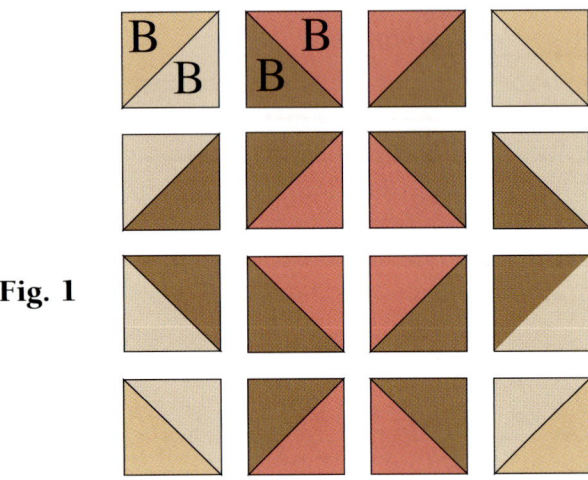

Fig. 1

Whether you piece by hand or machine, the seam allowances must all be ¼". After you have joined two pieces together, press the seams flat to one side—usually the darker side—not open.

Join the patches together in rows and again press the seam allowances to one side **(Fig. 2)**.

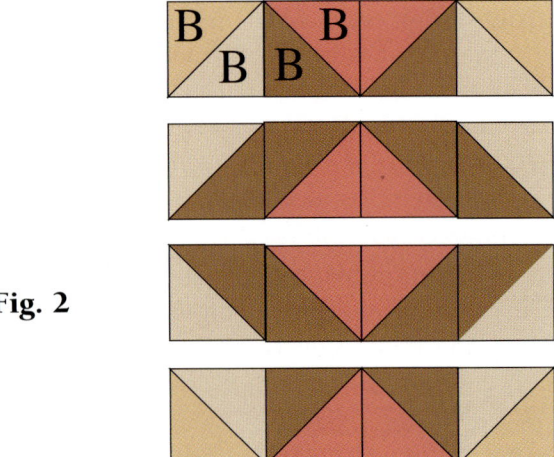

Fig. 2

After sewing the first row, press the seam allowances for the next rows in opposite directions. This will match seams that are crossed with other seams and will help eliminate any excess bulk **(Fig 3)**.

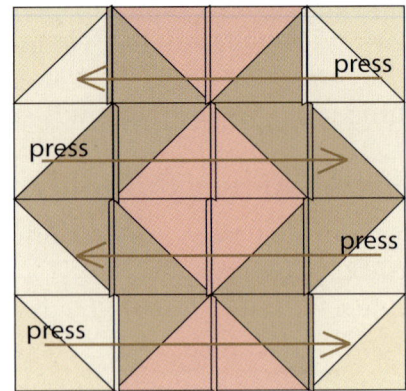

Fig. 3

Making a Potholder

Step One: Lay the chosen 9½" square of backing fabric on a flat surface wrong side up, and lay the three 9½" squares of batting on top.

Step Two: Very carefully, center the pieced patchwork block on the batting. Pin (or baste) the three layers together **(Fig. 4)**.

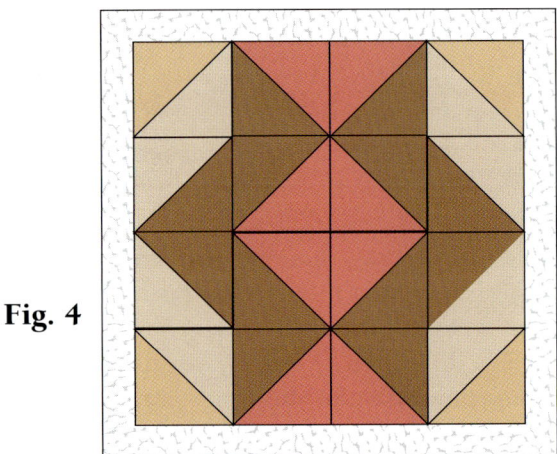

Fig. 4

Step Three: Quilt the five layers together either by hand or machine. The easiest method would be to "quilt in the ditch." This is a quilting technique in which the three pieces are joined together by stitching in the seams (the ditch) of the patchwork block with a neutral or matching cotton thread. Do not use nylon thread for quilting, as it will not withstand the heat.

Step Four: Fold one end of binding strip at a 45-degree angle. Cut along fold and press under ¼" **(Fig. 5)**.

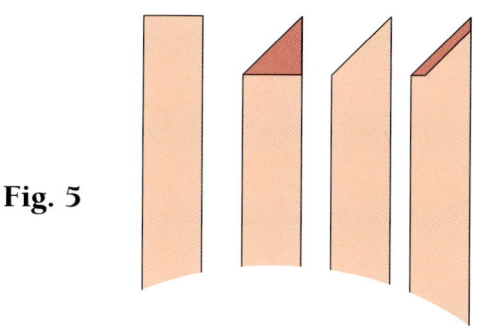

Fig. 5

Step Five: Fold the binding strip in half lengthwise, wrong sides together **(Fig. 6)**.

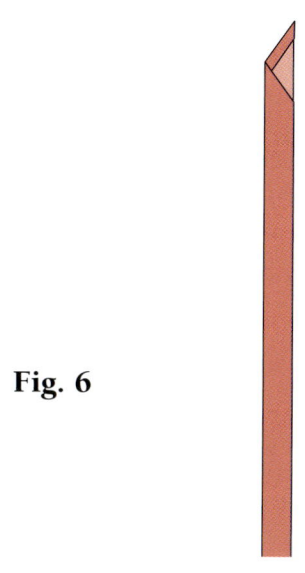

Fig. 6

Step Six: Matching the raw edges of the binding strip with the raw edge of the block, place the folded strip along one side. The backing and batting should not be covered **(Fig. 7)**.

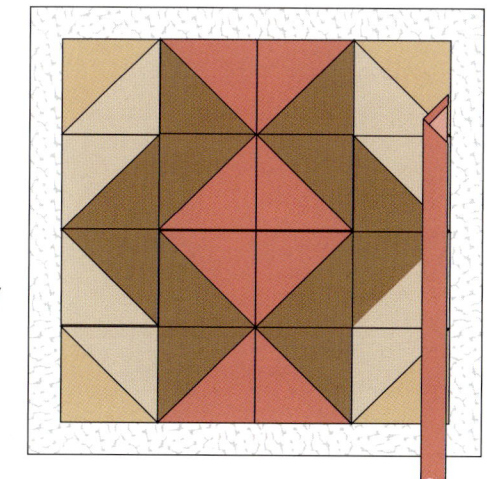

Fig. 7

Step Seven: Sew the strip to the block ¼" from the raw edge of the binding, beginning about 3" below the folded end of the binding. At the corner, stop ¼" from the edge of the pieced block and backstitch **(Fig. 8)**.

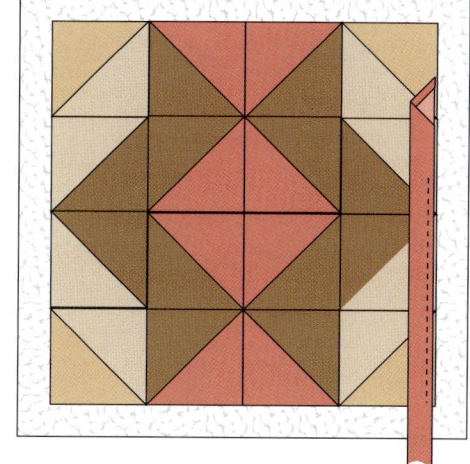

Fig. 8

Step Eight: Fold binding away from the block so it is at a right angle to the edge just sewn **(Fig. 9a)**. Then, fold the binding back on itself so the fold is on the block edge and the raw edges are aligned with the adjacent side of the block. Begin sewing at the block edge **(Fig. 9b)**.

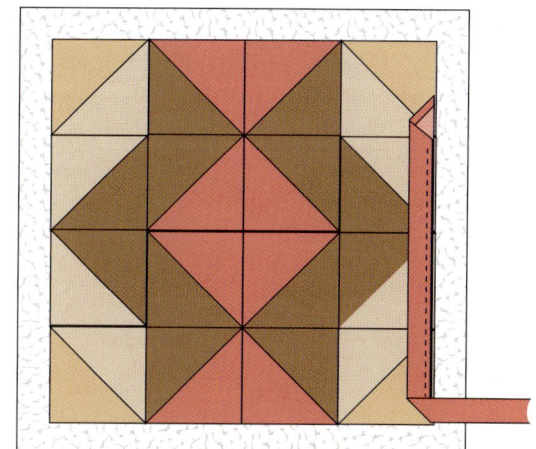

Fig. 9a

Fig. 9b

Step Nine: Continue in the same way around the remaining sides of the potholder. Stop about 2" away from the starting point. Trim any excess binding and tuck it inside the folded end. Finish the stitching **(Fig. 10)**.

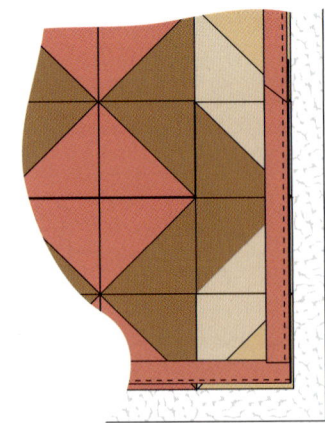

Fig. 10

Step Ten: Trim both the batting and the backing even with the edge of the quilt block.

Step Eleven: Fold the binding toward the back of the potholder so the seam line is covered; sew binding in place.

Step Twelve: If desired, sew the ring behind the upper left corner.

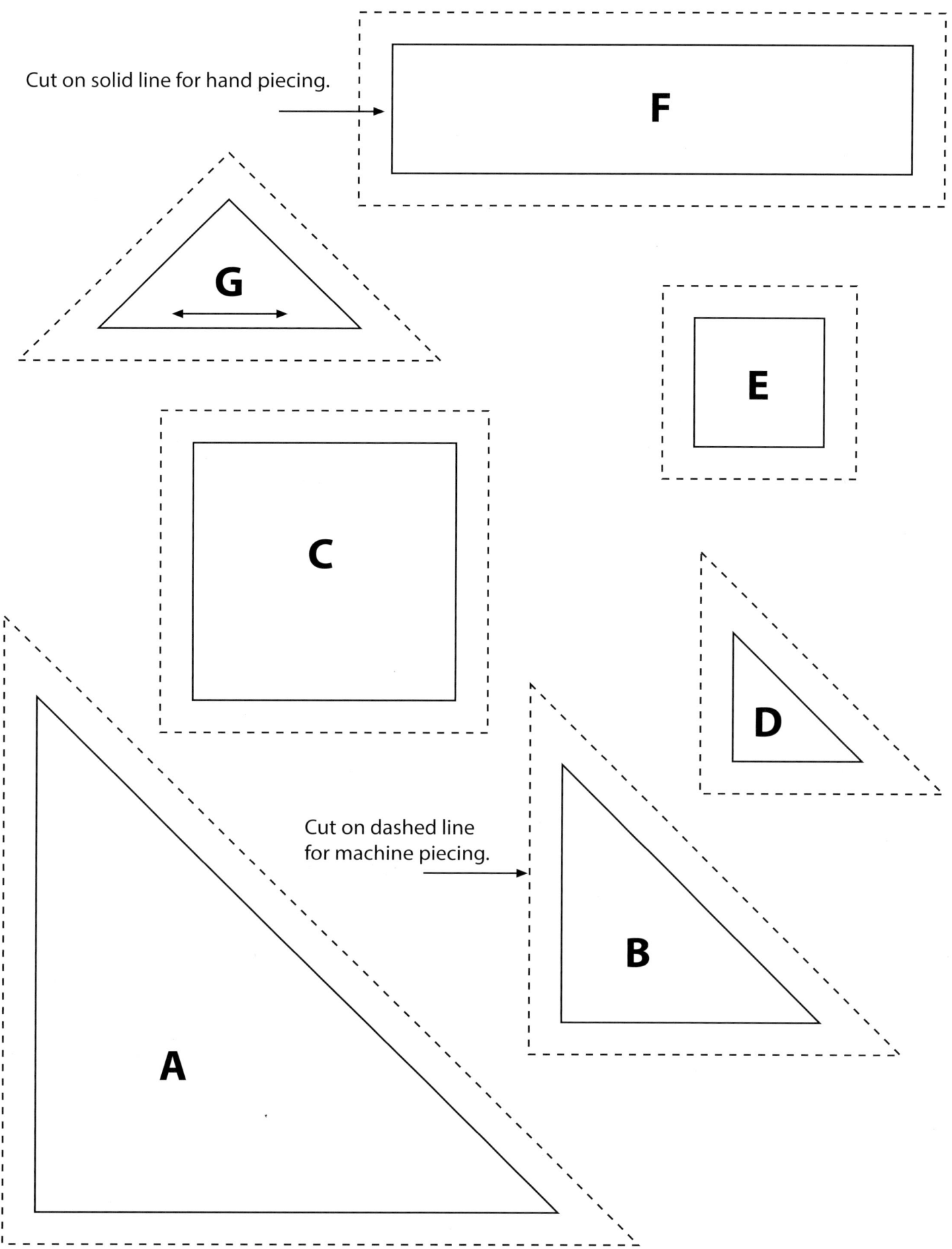

Index

Anna's Choice	6	Friendship	24	Ribbons	18
Anvil, The	7	Geometric	14	Road to Heaven	6
Apple Tree, The	7	Georgetown Circle	17	Road to Oklahoma	8
Arkansas Crossroads	5	Granny's Choice	41	Rocky Mountain Puzzle	9
Baby Bunting	33	Heart	30	Royal Star	11
Bachelor's Puzzle	5	Hither and Yon	38	Sailboat	8
Balkan Puzzle	40	Hole in the Barn Door	38	Shadow Boxes	50
Basket of Scraps	12	Hour Glass	10	Shoo-Fly	45
Blockade	11	Interwoven Puzzle	40	Shooting Squares	37
Brave World	17	Jack-in-the-Pulpit	28	Simple Flower Basket	16
Broken Dishes	26	Jacob's Ladder	50	Single Irish Chain	45
Butterfly, The	31	July Fourth	20	Snail's Trail	32
Buzzard's Roost	15	Kansas Dugout	42	Star of the West	55
Catch As You Can	29	King's Crown	49	Stars & Squares	4
Chevrons	18	Laurel Wreath	49	Stepping Stones	46
Chinese Puzzle	13	Lily	52	Streak of Lightning	58
Churn Dash	16	Linked Stars	57	Sugar Bowl	37
Clay's Choice	21	Lucky Pieces	48	Sunlight and Shadow	33
Coxey's Army	19	Mosaic	15	Sunny Lanes	39
Crazy Ann	35	Mrs. Smith's Favorite	10	Susannah	25
Criss Cross	44	Mrs. Taft's Choice	42	Tea Leaf	36
Crown and Star	43	Necktie	19	Thrift	4
Delectable Mountains	48	Nelson's Victory	58	Toad in the Puddle	44
Depression	30	Next-Door Neighbor	20	Totem	54
Devil's Claw	14	Noon and Night	24	Triangles and Stripes	29
Diamond Star	28	Northern Lights	13	Tulip	36
Double Pinwheel	47	Ocean Waves	53	Twelve Triangles	47
Double Quartet	41	Old Maid's Puzzle	12	Wheels	54
Eight-Pointed Star	25	Old Maid's Ramble	26	Whirlwind	43
Empire State	39	Original Block	46	White House Steps	52
Enclosed Stars	23	Patience Corners	27	Wild Goose Chase	22
End of Day	23	Pineapple	31	Wild Waves	35
End of the Road	57	Pinwheel Askew	56	Windblown Square	9
Eternal Triangle	22	Pinwheels	51	Windmill	51
Fancy Stripe	34	Railroad Crossing	27	Winged Star	56
Flower Basket	53	Return of the Swallows	21	Yankee Puzzle	34
Flying Fish	32	Ribbon Star	55		